900 J.G.
13140.

REFUGEES

Derek Heater

World Issues

A Divided World
Endangered Wildlife
Food or Famine?
Human Rights
International Terrorism
Nuclear Weapons
Population Growth
Refugees
The Arms Trade
The Energy Crisis
The Environment
The International Debt Crisis
The International Drugs Trade
World Health

Cover: Tibetan Children's Village run by Save the Children Fund in India
Frontispiece: Women collecting water at the Tugwajalle Refugee camp in Somalia

Editor: Jannet King
Series Designer: David Armitage

First published in 1988 by
Wayland (Publishers) Ltd,
61 Western Road, Hove
East Sussex, BN3 1JD, England

© Copyright 1988 Wayland (Publishers) Ltd

British Library Cataloguing in Publication Data

Heater, Derek, *1931–*
 Refugees.
 1. Refugees
 I. Title II. World issues
 325'.21

 ISBN 1-85210-436-8

Phototypeset by Kalligraphics Ltd, Redhill, Surrey
Printed and bound in Italy by Sagdos S.p.A., Milan

Contents

1. Introduction   6
2. Refugees in the past   8
3. Refugees today   15
4. Being a refugee   22
5. Help   30
6. Solutions?   39

Glossary   44

Books to read   45

Further information   45

Index   46

1 Introduction

Who are refugees?

Millions of people in the world today are homeless, depending on the charity and hospitality of others. Known as refugees, they are forced to try to make a home in a foreign country, while dreaming of returning to the land they belong to and which belongs to them. They, or their parents or even grandparents, have been forced to flee from their homes because of persecution, war or famine. They have chosen the uncertainty of homelessness to almost certain imprisonment, torture, starvation or death.

A refugee, in the words of the United Nations definition, is someone who,

> . . . owing to well-founded fear of being persecuted for reasons of race, religion, nationality, membership of a particular social group or political opinion, is outside the country of his nationality and is unable or, owing to such fear, is unwilling to avail himself of the protection of that country.

Sometimes individuals are forced to escape from their homeland; at other times, when conditions are particularly bad, fear seizes thousands of people who all flee together. Some refugees live in camps in countries which are neighbours of their own. A few find refuge in some of the richer countries, where they settle into new lives with homes and jobs.

Where and how many?

Who are these unfortunate people? Which countries and areas of the world are most affected? Most of the refugees in the world today are from five areas: Central America, the Middle East, eastern, central and southern parts of Africa, Afghanistan and South East Asia. These are shown in the map below. The map also shows you where most of the refugees have gone. Countries labelled in capital letters

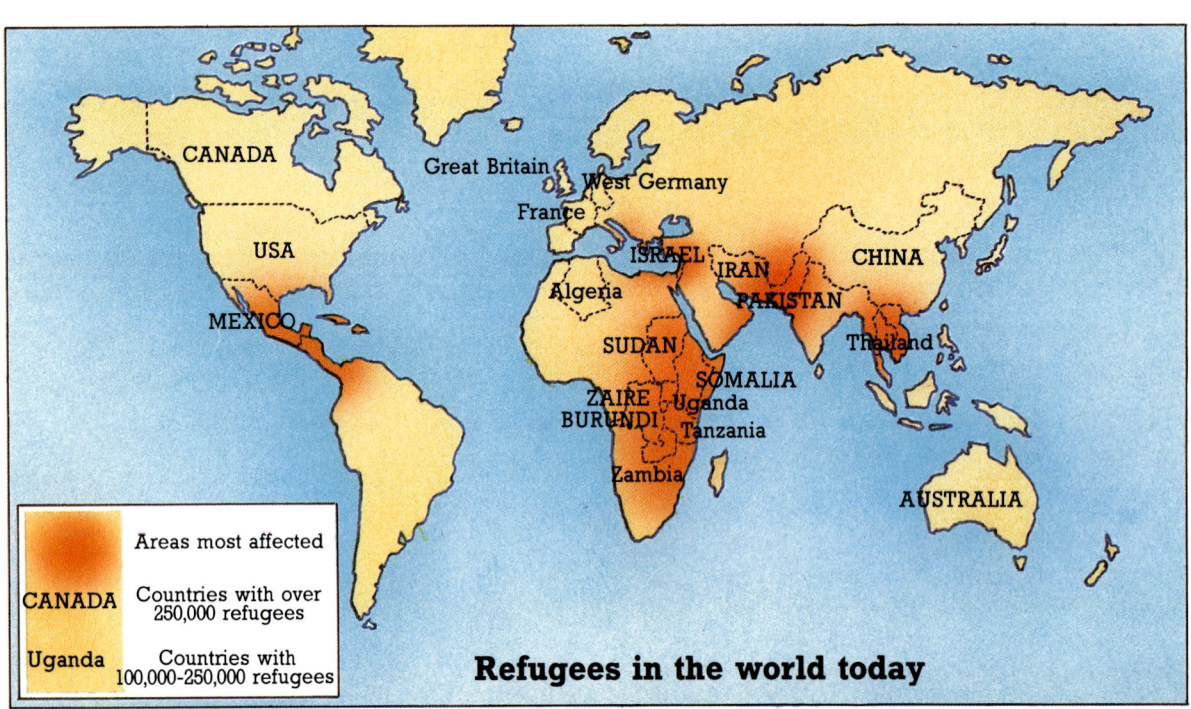

Refugees in the world today

have taken over 250,000; those in small letters have between 100,000 and 250,000. By far the biggest burdens have been borne by Pakistan and Iran. In 1986 they had five million refugees between them, the equivalent of the population of Scotland. This was perhaps a third or more of all the world's refugees, which has been estimated at 15 million (the equivalent of the population of Australia).

Apart from the colossal sum of human misery suffered by refugees, these numbers mean a huge outlay of money just to provide them with

Many refugees leave their homes because of drought and famine. These Ethiopian children are in a Sudanese camp.

the bare minimum of shelter, food and sanitation. The costs are borne by various international and charitable organizations and by the countries (often themselves very poor) to which the refugees flee. It is a dreadful reflection of the state of our world that so many human beings have been deprived of their homes and homelands.

2 Refugees in the past

Origin of the word

The word 'refugee' was first used 300 years ago. In the 1680s King Louis XIV of France started to persecute the Protestant people of France, the Huguenots. They suffered great cruelties and were forbidden to worship in the way they wished. A law was passed which forbade them from leaving France; anyone caught would be sent to row Mediterranean galleys –

Joseph, Mary and the baby Jesus fleeing to Egypt to escape persecution by Herod. The picture is by the sixteenth-century Italian painter, Jacopo Bassano.

in effect, to become slaves. But hundreds of thousands – nearly one fifth of the total population of France – risked this fate and managed to escape abroad.

This is how the French philosopher, Voltaire, described what happened:

> In the course of three years nearly fifty thousand families left the kingdom and were afterwards followed by still more. They brought with them to foreign countries their arts, their manufactures, their wealth. . . . A whole quarter of London was populated with French silk operatives; others brought to that city the perfected art of glass-cutting, an art that was henceforth lost to France.

Voltaire loathed religious intolerance, so perhaps he exaggerated a little. However, this quotation is helpful in reminding us that refugees can bring important benefits to the countries where they settle.

Some famous refugees

There were, of course, plenty of refugees well before there was a word to describe them. For example, the founders of two of the world's great religions were refugees. Soon after he was born Jesus Christ was taken by his parents to a foreign country to escape being killed. This is how St Matthew described the event:

> . . . the angel of the Lord appeareth to Joseph in a dream, saying, Arise, and take the young child and his mother, and flee into Egypt, and be then there until I bring thee word: for Herod will seek the young child to destroy him.

622 years later, the founder of Islam, the Prophet Muhammad, fled with some of his followers from their city of Makkah. They went to a place which was later called Al Madinah. The Arabic word for this flight to Al Madinah is *Hejira*. The day is still taken as the start of the Muslim year.

In more recent times there have been other famous refugees. In 1933 the mathematical genius Einstein fled to the USA from Berlin when the Nazis started harassing Jewish people. And in 1940, the great composer Béla Bartók also fled to the USA.

Europe between the World Wars

Wars often create refugees. People try to escape from advancing armies to avoid being raped, injured or killed, or because their houses and farms are destroyed in the battles. These problems affected millions of people during both World Wars, especially in Europe.

After the First World War an international organization called the League of Nations was created. The League decided to help refugees and appointed a Norwegian, Fridtjof Nansen, as High Commissioner with this responsibility. He was a remarkable man who had become a national hero as an Arctic explorer. He had been the first to cross Greenland and had later travelled nearer to the North Pole than anyone before him. Then he had entered politics and helped his country to gain its independence from Sweden. During the Russian Civil War of 1920–21 there was dreadful famine and Nansen organized food supplies to save at least some people from starvation. He was awarded the

These Armenian refugees were photographed in 1918 in a refugee camp probably in Iran. They had been fortunate enough to have escaped the fate of up to a million Armenians who had been massacred by Turkish troops.

Three Jewish refugees waiting at Liverpool Street Station in London for their relatives to claim them. In one week in July 1939 400 young Jews arrived in Britain from Germany and Austria.

Nobel Peace Prize for this work. Nansen believed passionately in international co-operation. He set up the 'Nansen International Certificates' as a kind of international passport for refugees until they could find a country in which to settle.

In 1933, three years after Nansen's death, the League of Nations set up a special office in London to cope with the growing problem of refugees from Germany. The Nazi persecution of the Jews, which eventually led to 6 million being killed, was getting under way. At first Jews were merely excluded from certain professions in Germany. Their lives seemed not to be in danger. But in 1938 the Nazi persecution took an uglier turn: synagogues, shops and homes were attacked. In panic many Jews sought safety in other lands. Some went to Palestine, some to the USA, some to Britain.

To Britain came the 'children's transports'. One parent from each family was allowed to bid farewell at the railway station. Most were never reunited. Jewish refugees in Britain were given little help by the British government. They had to depend on the kindness and sympathy of individuals to help them start a new life.

> There are very few of us nowadays who can manage to avoid having our attention drawn to 'the refugee problem'. . . .
> We see pictures of even tiny children arriving at our ports, labelled like parcels, bundles of forlorn and helpless childhood, homeless, parentless, seeking refuge and sanctuary from the storm of cruelty and oppression which has swept their parents to penury, imprisonment, torture, death.
> *An account by a British Woman who worked for Save the Children Fund and Child Refugees*

The destruction of millions of houses across Europe forced the survivors to leave their towns and villages and seek shelter elsewhere.

Post-War Europe

The human misery and chaos caused by the Second World War is difficult to imagine. Aerial bombardment and fighting across much of Europe destroyed millions of homes. Huge areas of some cities, especially in Germany and Russia, ceased to exist. Millions of soldiers were captured as prisoners of war. Many civilians left their homes, or what remained of them, in the wake of the battling armies. Others had been transported hundreds of miles from their homes by the Germans to concentration camps or to work as slave labour in factories. Then, to make matters worse, the frontiers of several countries in central and eastern Europe were changed. For instance, Russians and Poles moved in to land that had once been German, and some Germans fled to the western part of their country.

Not all of these 'displaced persons' were refugees. Some, for example the prisoners of war and slave labourers, could return to their own countries. But Europe had never before in its history experienced such a massive movement of people as occurred from 1945 to 1948. One estimate is that 30 million people moved from one country to another, but it may have been nearer 50 million. It was quite impossible to keep accurate records in such confusion.

The largest group of post-war European displaced persons were the Germans. Probably some 12 million were uprooted and wandered westwards to what is now West Germany. It is possible to divide these refugees into four groups:

1. Those who fled from the advancing Allied armies during the closing months of the war.
2. Families who had lived (some for centuries) in various east European countries. They were now hated and expelled.
3. People expelled from the eastern parts of Germany now taken over by Poland. Polish people were moved into these lands to replace them.
4. Those in what is now East Germany who did not want to live in a Communist state. Hundreds of thousands of people continued to flee from East Germany each year until 1961 when the Berlin Wall was built to stop them.

In the years immediately after the war Germany was divided into four zones of occupation, administered by the Soviet Union, the USA, Britain and France. At first the armies of the three western allies had to cope with the problem of

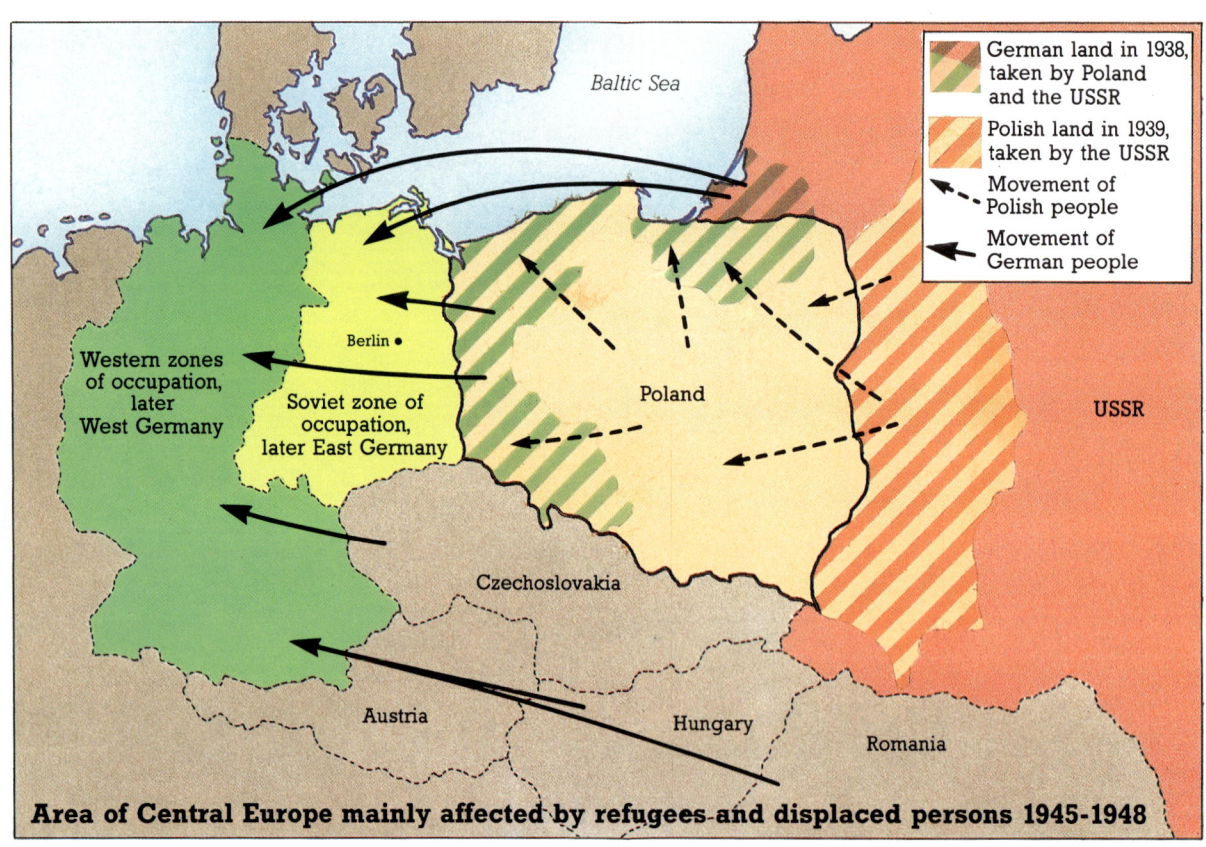

Area of Central Europe mainly affected by refugees and displaced persons 1945-1948

finding homes for the German refugees. The Supreme Headquarters Allied Expeditionary Force (SHAEF) established a Displaced Persons Division. From 1943 to 1947 the civilian organization UNRRA (United Nations Relief and Rehabilitation Administration) handled the problems of the people from the Allied countries who had fought against the Axis powers in Europe (Germany and Italy). In 1947 the United Nations set up the International Refugee Organization (IRO) to care for refugees. Throughout central Europe thousands of camps had to be organized to shelter and feed all these homeless people. IRO also tried to arrange for the refugees to travel to new homelands, or back to their old if they wished to return. The people who ran these camps had enormous problems such as how to find enough food and how to communicate without a knowledge of foreign languages.

As this contemporary cartoon shows, refugees from East Germany were not always welcomed by prosperous West Germans.

The Far East

In 1947 Britain gave independence to India, which had been part of the British Empire. The majority of Indians were Hindu, though there were large numbers of Muslims in the north-west and north-east of the sub-continent. Some Muslims were afraid that the Hindus would control independent India and so they asked that the country should be partitioned to create a mainly Muslim Pakistan and a mainly Hindu India. But it is impossible to draw precise frontiers between states according to where people live. Therefore millions of Hindus found themselves in Pakistan, and millions of Muslims in India.

Many were frightened about what would happen to them if they stayed in the 'wrong' country. In fact, killings soon started and millions of terrified people started to travel, some by train, some on foot. No one knows quite how many people took flight – probably 6 or 7 million Hindus and Sikhs to India and the same number of Muslims to Pakistan. Hundreds of thousands of these refugees were massacred on their journeys.

> I think of the poor refugee in Delhi, in both East Punjab [India] and West Punjab [Pakistan] today while it is raining. I have heard that a convoy 57 miles long is pouring into [India] from West Punjab. It makes my brain reel to think that such can be. Such a thing is unparalleled in the history of the world, and it makes me, as it should make you, hang my head in shame.
> *Mahatma Gandhi, at a prayer meeting in 1947*

In the other large Asian country, China, many millions also became refugees, though over a longer period of time. There were three reasons for this: the war with Japan (1937–45), the Communist Revolution, and the most terrible famine in the early 1960s in which over 15 million people died. Some of these refugees fled to nearby places, especially Hong Kong and the island of Taiwan. It is estimated that between 1949 and 1962 on average more than 60,000 Chinese people entered Hong Kong each year.

The problem revived

By about 1960 the huge numbers of refugees created by the events of the 1940s had subsided. The United Nations was nevertheless still so concerned by the problem that it designated 1959 World Refugee Year. In this way it helped to draw attention to the needs of the estimated 1.2 million refugees in the world. At the time that number seemed horrific. During the years since then the number has increased more than tenfold.

Some of the millions of Sikhs and Hindus who, in 1947, fled from their homes in what was to become Pakistan. On the road they would have passed Muslim refugees travelling in the opposite direction, out of India, towards Pakistan.

3 Refugees today

Reasons for the refugee problem today

The scale of human suffering in the present century is a disgrace to mankind. Wars have caused the slaughter of scores of millions of people. Brutal governments have imprisoned, tortured, maimed and killed millions more in attempts to crush criticism and opposition. Still more millions have died of starvation because governments have interfered with the way peasants have cultivated the land or because of the destruction of crops in war.

There is little doubt that fanaticism has made this catalogue of people's inhumanity to other people so horrendous, long and blood-stained. Human life and dignity have been cheaply priced because political or religious beliefs have been held more dear.

When these conditions become intolerable people often try to escape to preserve their freedom and their lives. In our own century scores of millions of people have chosen to leave their homes and to seek refuge for fear of the fate that would befall them if they stayed. Most countries in the world today are affected by the refugee problem, either because people have fled from them or because refugees have found protection and hospitality there. In this chapter we shall look at five examples and try to understand what has caused people to become refugees from their homelands in each case.

Palestinians

From ancient times until 1948 the Jewish people had no country of their own. Then, about a hundred years ago, some Jews began to dream of returning to their old homeland of Palestine.

After the gruesome suffering of the Jews at the hands of the Nazis, it was agreed that they should have part of Palestine as their own state of Israel. In 1948 it is estimated that there were about 700,000 Jews and 1,300,000 Arabs in Palestine. In that year the United Nations drew

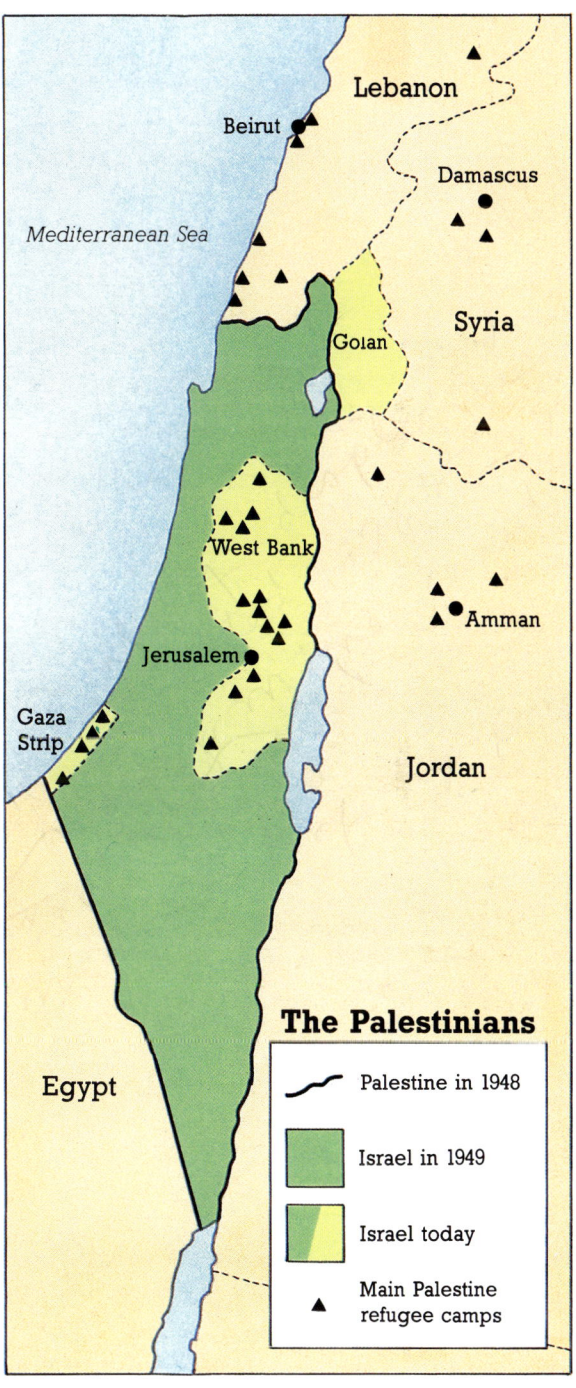

up a plan to partition the country. The new state of Israel came into existence but immediately war broke out between it and its Arab neighbours. Hundreds of thousands of the Palestinian Arabs fled, became refugees, and they and their families have remained so ever since.

Why was this? Israelis and Arabs disagree.

> The Arab refugee problem was caused by a war of aggression, launched by the Arab States against Israel in 1947 and 1948. Let there be no mistake. If there had been no war against Israel, with its consequent harvest of bloodshed, misery, panic and flight, there would have been no problem of Arab refugees today. Once you determine the responsibility for that war, you have determined the responsibility for the refugee problem.
> *Abba Eban, Israeli representive at the United Nations, 1958*

> All wars create refugees, and after the armies have departed the peasants and merchants return to take up their lives again. Civilized Governments accept that they have a responsibility for those who live in the land they rule. But after the armistice agreements of 1949 Israel refused – with limited exceptions – to allow the Arab refugees to return.
> *Albert Hourani, Arab scholar*

When the Palestinians fled in 1948 they scattered to many countries. A number settled in camps in the Gaza Strip and the West Bank (see map). But when another war broke out in 1967 and Israel occupied these two areas, many families fled yet again. As we shall see in Chapter 5 a United Nations organization (UNRWA) was set up to look after the Palestinian refugees.

Beach Camp, Gaza, run by UNRWA. Some of the Palestinians have lived there for forty years.

In 1987 they were still caring for nearly 300,000 people in camps in Jordan, Syria, Lebanon, Gaza and the West Bank and almost 900,000 more outside the camps. A quarter of the total population of Jordan in 1987 were refugees. About 3 million more Palestinians were living away from their homeland but without the legal status of refugees cared for by UNRWA.

For forty years, therefore, millions of Palestinians have lived away from the country they think of as their homeland. Nor is there much hope even now of a solution to their problems, for both Israeli Jews and Palestinian Arabs claim the same country as their own. Few other refugees in the world today have had to endure their plight with such helpless patience as the Palestinians.

Vietnamese 'boat' people

If the Palestinians hold the record for the length of time they have been refugees, the Vietnamese have suffered from war more intensely than any other people since 1945. First they fought against the French for independence. The country was partitioned. Then the Communist Vietnamese in the north fought against the non-Communists in the south. Then the Americans fought against the Communists until in 1973 they admitted defeat and withdrew. Two years later the Communists of North Vietnam took over the south and reunited the country. They persecuted many of the middle-class people in Ho Chi Minh City and other towns partly because they wished to introduce economic changes along Communist lines and partly because many of the prosperous traders and industrialists were Chinese and not native

South East Asia

Many of the refugees from Indo-China end up in closed camps such as Chi Ma Wan in Hong Kong. The high fence is to prevent the refugees leaving the camp because the authorities want to resettle them in an organized way.

Vietnamese. The sufferings of these people were made more acute in 1977 when weather conditions led to a disastrous shortage of food.

Families tried to escape, many by sea. By the end of 1977 an average of 1,500 people were leaving by boat each month. They often paid fishermen large sums of money for boats which were barely seaworthy. Crammed in dangerous numbers into these rickety craft, they set sail for the open sea. Some perished in attacks by pirates or as their frail boats sank in stormy waters. The fortunate ones reached land in friendly countries or were picked up by passing ships. Many of the hundreds of thousands who survived the ordeal were resettled in countries of the West, though thousands of others still languish in refugee camps throughout South East Asia, such as in Hong Kong, awaiting a permanent home.

Central America

Many of the countries of Central America are very poor. Most have been ruled by dictators and in recent years have been torn apart by revolutions and civil wars. These conflicts have caused tens of thousands to become refugees, especially from Guatemala, El Salvador and Nicaragua. Most have escaped to Honduras and Mexico. United Nations volunteers patrol the borders of Honduras, leading refugees to the safety of reception centres and then to the refugee camps. In 1987 there were over 300,000 refugees in Central America.

Afghanistan

Afghanistan is a mountainous country in central Asia tucked between the Soviet Union, Iran and Pakistan. In 1979 there was political upheaval in the country and the Soviet Union sent troops to support the Communist government. For centuries the Afghanis have been devout Muslims. They are renowned for their dislike of foreign invaders and their willingness to fight. It is not surprising therefore that the invasion of the foreign atheist Russian forces prompted many to take to the rugged hills,

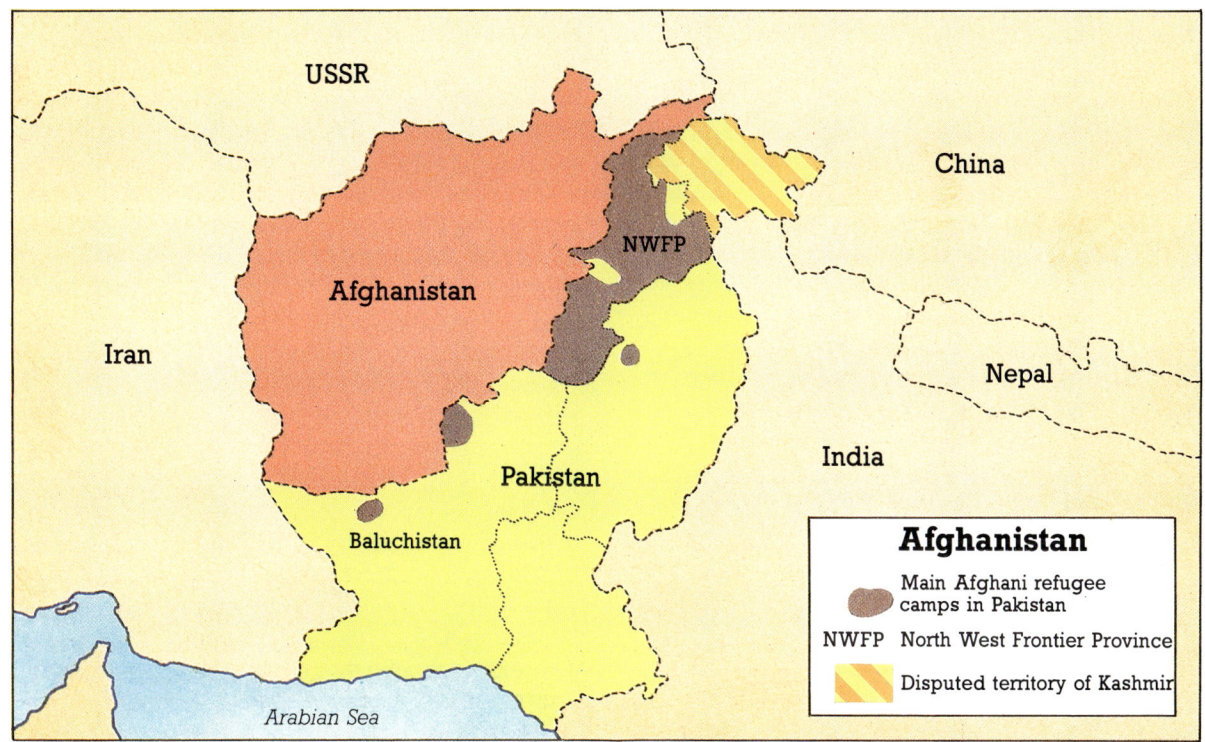

band themselves together into guerrilla armies, and fight the hated invaders. The struggle has been bitterly fought. In a desperate effort to preserve their religion and their lives enormous numbers of refugees have fled to the safety of neighbouring Iran and Pakistan. In the space of six years nearly 5 million streamed across the frontiers.

As a result of this massive exodus, Pakistan has the largest refugee population of any country in the world – nearly 3 million by 1986 (almost the equivalent of the entire population of New Zealand). In order to accommodate them 320 special refugee villages have been established. The presence of such a vast refugee population is, of course, a huge problem for Pakistan. The weight of this human burden has been indicated in the following way by a senior Pakistani official:

> There are many places in Pakistan where the size of the refugee population exceeds the size of the local population. The pressures in these areas have been immense. There is a shortage of land and drinking water, grazing facilities for livestock are limited. So obviously the presence of the refugees has led to a tremendous burden on these limited resources. Even the forests were seriously damaged in the initial stages. . . . I feel that our people have demonstrated tremendous accommodation for the refugees and have shared their limited resources very generously.

An Afghani woman cooking over an open fire in Bababer camp near Peshawar in Pakistan.

There has nevertheless been heated resentment which sparked into angry violence, for example in 1986 when Pakistani officials tried to break up a drug smuggling organization among the refugees. In the fierce fighting that ensued as many as 200 Pakistanis were killed. The Afghani refugees have weapons because the guerrillas use some of the refugee camps as bases from which to make raids across the border against the Communist armies in Afghanistan.

Africa

Half the world's refugees today are in Africa and many African countries are affected by political conflict, civil wars and famine. Over the past quarter of a century, as violence has flared and food supplies have failed, the number of human beings who have fled stricken regions has mounted. It is this combination of fighting and famine that has made the condition of many millions of African refugees uniquely pitiful.

This fate may be symbolized by the sufferings in the 1980s of the people of Ethiopia whose plight has been widely publicized in the news media.

How did this crisis arise? Since 1960 there have been a number of civil wars in several parts of the country, but mainly in the northern provinces of Eritrea and Tigre, where liberation movements have been fighting for independence or autonomy. Most of the country is, moreover, poor and rugged. The peasants depend on an uncertain rainfall to grow their crops and water their livestock. In 1973 the rains failed. They failed even more disastrously several seasons running in the early 1980s and fighting in the northern parts of this geographically isolated country made conditions even worse: in some areas it was dangerous for farmers to plant crops or for relief supplies to be brought to the starving. A member of the Ethiopian government at the time has recalled the connection between the starvation and the civil war:

> The months between March and December, 1984, were the most terrible the people of northern and central Ethiopia had ever seen. . . . Hundreds of thousands abandoned their homes, . . . selling everything they owned to wander off in search of food. . . . Hunger and war were intertwined and the most seriously affected areas were Eritrea, Tigre and Wollo – the areas where the major insurgent movements operate.

Ethiopia
Areas most affected by drought, 1984-85
Provinces most affected by civil war
← Refugees

Hundreds of thousands of families moved, or were moved by the government. Some became refugees in the neighbouring countries of Sudan, Somalia or Djibouti. Others were forcibly resettled in other parts of Ethiopia. By 1986 there were over half a million Ethiopian refugees in Sudan and 700,000 in Somalia. Even the easing of the famine by that year complicated the problem, for 300,000 people returned

A few of the 700,000 Ethiopian refugees in Somalia. These are in a camp run by Save the Children Fund.

to Ethiopia to take up life again in their own country, but were still refugees from their original villages.

Although the sufferings of the Ethiopians have been well publicized, they must not blind us to the agonies of other African peoples. Indeed, very few African countries are unaffected. The related problems of South Africa and Mozambique are so serious that a few words must be said about them. The South African apartheid system of treating black people as inferior to whites has, naturally, caused distress and anger among black people, and provoked the hostility of nearly the whole world to the white minority government. The police have arrested people suspected of opposing the government and many have been imprisoned, badly treated and even killed. Thousands of black South Africans have fled to neighbouring countries. Millions more have stayed on, a silent majority.

In the meantime civil war has been raging in the neighbouring country of Mozambique. The forces fighting against the Mozambican government are supported by the South African government. The fierce conflict has caused hundreds of thousands of people to flee their homes in fear. To the death and destruction of war have been added the miseries of famine as drought has afflicted many regions of the country.

Children (and old people) are the first to suffer from under-nourishment. This little boy has just arrived at a camp in Sudan after a long journey.

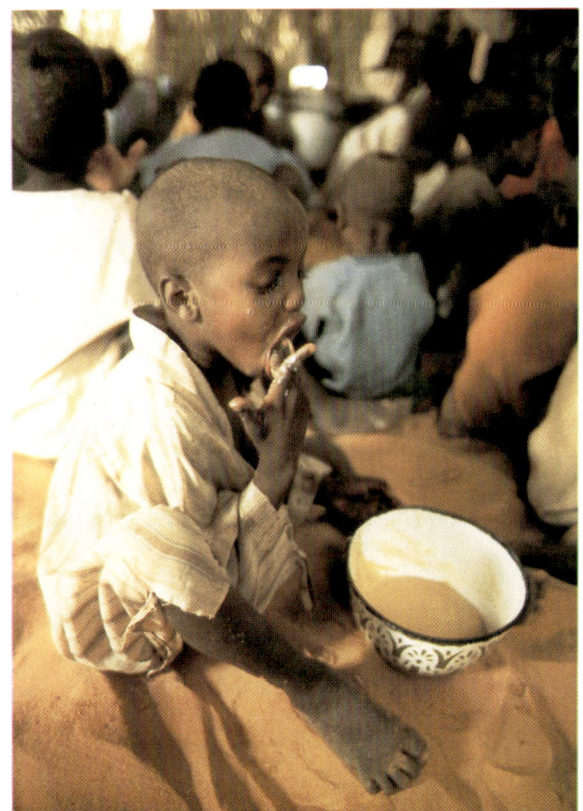

4 Being a refugee

Flight to safety

The previous chapter contained many figures and facts about recent political history. These are important for understanding why the problem is so serious. But what does it feel like to be a refugee? What are a refugee's fears, miseries and hopes?

Imagine the confusion of thoughts in the mind of a refugee. The first emotion is fear. Flight to another land involves surrendering so much that gives meaning to life – often everything except safety and life itself. Such a decision is not taken lightly. A refugee is someone who has been forced to abandon his or her home for fear of the consequences of staying. This fear may be a calculated estimate of the risk of remaining, or it may be a panic reaction to rumours. Most refugees feel a terrible wrench at leaving the homes that they and their families have lived in for many years. They probably have to leave behind all their belongings except the oddments they can carry on their journey, which may be long and tiring. They will also have to leave behind old or sick relatives who cannot cope with the journey. Small wonder that some refugees feel anger or hatred for those responsible for their destitution and misery. If they see little hope of returning to their homeland or of settling into an acceptable life-style in another land, then a mood of despair may well deepen their wretchedness, fuelled partly by home-sickness, and partly by shame at the loss of self-respect because of their dependence on charity for food, clothing and shelter.

> We had to escape. . . . When we finally arrived here in Somalia they called us 'refugees'. That means 'beggar' in our language. It is awful to be a beggar and live in a camp. We are nothing any more. Only numbers.
>
> When I think about my life back home, it feels like thousands of insects crawling around under my skin and then it is impossible to sleep.
>
> *A 14-year-old Ethiopian girl*

This Ethiopian family has travelled many miles to reach the relative safety of a camp in Sudan.

In addition to all these general miseries, women and children endure their own particular kinds of suffering. Although it is almost always men who create the climate of fear that forces people to become refugees, there are more women than men refugees in the world. In some camps there are so few men that women must undertake unfamiliar men's jobs and be in charge of the family. Yet many governments are unwilling to give women official refugee status or talk to them about their needs. The children who suffer most are, of course, the orphans: they have lost their parents as well as their homes.

The first stage of becoming a refugee is the journey to a place of safety. The journey itself is often hazardous. Refugees trying to cross a well-guarded frontier or coast run two kinds of danger. They may risk arrest or death at the hands of their own security forces, or being returned to their own country by the authorities of the country in which they had hoped for sanctuary. For example, some of the Vietnamese 'boat people' were intercepted by their own government's ships. In Europe, the 'Iron Curtain' frontier between the Communist countries in the east and western Europe is heavily guarded on the eastern side. A number of would-be refugees have been stopped, for instance, at the notorious Berlin Wall, which has divided that city since 1961.

Women do much of the heavy work in the fields at the camps for Guatemalans in Mexico.

The Vietnamese people who flee from persecution often face even greater danger from drowning in small and overcrowded boats. These refugees have been rescued by the French organization, Médecins du Monde.

However, for most refugees the peril of the journey lies in the environment. In tropical countries, trudging for days in search of a place of sanctuary may well cause exhaustion or starvation. The television cameras have shown the world the pathetic lines of emaciated Ethiopians making their way painfully through their parched land. Some – the weak and the children especially – succumb.

The following description of dangers encountered by Mozambicans seeking refuge in a black-populated area of South Africa provides a vivid illustration of the nerve-racking and tantalising gap between flight and safety.

> Early in the morning of 19 February, a group of 12 footsore men come limping into the camp. They have been walking some five days. . . . Crossing [the Kruger Park] is no mean feat. Not only must the refugees avoid lions, cheetahs and leopards, but also the game wardens and South African security police. Up to 2,000 Mozambicans a month are caught by South African authorities and handed back across the border.

Even if the country of their destination is basically friendly, the authorities may well bar them from entry. Destitute foreign refugees are often unwelcome.

Because few refugees enjoy the chance of taking with them much in the way of wealth or personal possessions, reception camps must provide all the basic necessities. Tents or crude huts afford some shelter from the heat, the cold or the rain. Simple clothing and blankets are needed for protection, and, of course, food and water are essential. The various governments, international and charitable organizations which run these camps provide the bare minimum, for these are transit centres, from which, as soon as possible, the refugees are conveyed to camps or settlements. In times of specially tense crises some of these centres

Delousing of clothes and bodies helps to keep the camps as hygienic as possible, so as to prevent the spread of disease.

can become overcrowded and squalid. Sanitation and health care become serious problems. For instance, one camp in Somalia in the mid-1980s had to struggle to cope with thousands of Ethiopian refugees. When cholera broke out, the plans to transport them to a new camp had to be postponed for fear that the disease might spread. One official described the camp as 'hell on earth'.

Most refugees stay in transit centres only briefly. Then they are registered officially as refugees and are conveyed to camps where the facilities are a little better and where more permanent shelters are constructed.

Life in a camp

The organization of a refugee camp is no easy matter. It is like creating a village in a very short space of time. The site must have water for drinking, cooking and cleanliness. It must have a road or track so that supplies such as food and medicines can be transported to the camp. Buildings must be constructed – for homes mainly, but a medical centre and later a school are also required. Furthermore, it is important that the men especially be able to work. This is partly to help earn a living for their families and partly so that they feel useful. Fertile fields are therefore necessary for growing food and workshops for light crafts.

> In Somalia since 1979 thousands of people have been living in refugee camps. Mainly nomadic people who fled from Ethiopia, they were used to a high-protein diet of meat and camel's milk. In the camps they have had to switch to relief food – mainly maize flour, rice, tea and sugar. . . . The children in particular find the change of diet difficult.
>
> *Oxfam report*

Water is one of the most important facilities in a camp, not only for drinking, but for washing.

At a Mexican camp for Guatemalans, the refugees build their own houses.

Not all camps meet these requirements. Sometimes the earth is barren; sometimes water has to be brought in tankers. Life in such poorly provided camps remains harsh. The refugee's hope of a tolerable existence may be brutally disappointed. The misery of unfortunate refugees may also be aggravated by the upheaval of removal to yet another camp. This may be because of attacks across the frontier putting the refugees' lives in danger, or because the local inhabitants object to the refugees living nearby, or because a better camp has been prepared.

Even so, many refugees manage to settle and build up their lives again. With the help of the organizations described in Chapter 5, children are given a basic education. Adults are helped with tools and seeds to grow food, tend livestock and make clothes and furniture for their daily lives. They are also helped to sell their goods or to find work in the local community.

As an example of quite successful camps let us take a look at those organized in southern Mexico for refugees from Guatemala. In the early 1980s over 40,000 Guatemalans fled because of the civil war in their country and settled in camps just over the border. But because of attacks on the camps from Guatemala, in 1984 many of the refugees were sent to new, safe camps. Two years later an American expert on refugee problems was able to report:

> Tremendous progress has been made since the first of more than 18,000 Guatemalan refugees were transferred to the new settlements from camps close to Mexico's border with its southern neighbour. Neat houses line the settlement's broad paths, bright-eyed children chase chickens and piglets, women nurse their infants and the men work long hours on the land that the Mexican Government has provided for the refugees.

The 18,000 refugees were organized into four settlements. Each of these communities was given land, tools, seed and livestock. Some progress was soon made towards achieving the Mexican authorities' aim of making the settlements self-sufficient. In addition, although the Guatemalans were peasant farmers, some have been retrained in carpentry, tailoring and baking. Others have been employed on basic wages on the local sugar plantations and in sugar-processing plants.

Some of the refugees have become contented with the secure life of the camps, but others pine for the life they left behind. The Mexican plain is no real substitute for the Guatemalan highlands, nor the drab refugee garments for their colourful clothes. As the months and years roll by they are slowly losing the local languages and customs they once cherished, though the children are taught a little about these in the schools. Yet few even of those who feel most uncomfortable in their new surroundings dare risk returning.

Refugees in the Mexican camps are encouraged to practise traditional crafts so that their skills don't die out.

The Baqa's Camp for Palestinians in Jordan provides basic, but cheerless, accommodation.

Settling down

None of the thousands of camps around the world was ever intended to be permanent. And yet, even after living in camps for forty years, many Palestinians still have no hope of any other kind of life. They still dream of returning to their original towns and villages and cannot think of their camps as real homes. Here is a typical story, written in a British newspaper in 1987:

> To Abu Shinab and his family, home isn't Jordan, where they've lived for the twenty years since the Six-Day War. Home isn't even the pink house in Rafah refugee camp in the Gaza Strip, where they lived for most of another twenty years after the 1948 war. . . . Home to them and their children is a farm and a village in the south of Israel. . . . Abu Shinab says life in Moka Camp. . . . is all right. . . . He has a small business, a tiny room off the mud street where he presses clothes. . . . His wife cuts in angrily on this well-rehearsed piece of good manners. Life is not all right, she says, they have neither space nor money enough to live decently.

For such Palestinians none of the three ways of ceasing to be refugees is possible. The first is repatriation, that is returning to their homeland. The second is finding work, making a new home, settling in the country of asylum, and perhaps becoming a citizen of that country. The third possibility is resettling overseas and becoming a citizen of another country willing to accept them. Let us take each of these in turn.

Naturally many refugees wish to return to their homeland whenever it is possible and safe to do so. In recent years hundreds of thousands have been able to resume their lives in this way. In Africa voluntary repatriation often takes place. In some cases people have fled more because of temporary famine than any long-lasting political or religious persecution and conflict. For example, in the mid-1980s nearly half a million Ethiopians returned to their homeland from camps in Somalia and Djibouti, despite the fact that it was still suffering the effects of drought.

Africa is also the continent where a large proportion of the refugees have given up any

Some refugees are accepted by Western countries. They may take time to adapt to their new surroundings but many are taken to special centres where they are taught about the local culture. These Vietnamese women are gaining useful experience in the shops.

host government makes land available and the United Nations and other international organizations provide food, tools, seeds and livestock. The refugees then set about building their homes and making a village community. In this way scores of thousands of Namibians have settled in Angola, Ugandans in Sudan and Rwandans in Tanzania. For refugees who wish to settle in towns, conditions are much harder because of the high levels of overcrowding and unemployment.

Settlement in a town can be easier if a refugee has managed to obtain entry to a wealthy industrial country. One of the countries with the proudest record of hospitality is Canada. As early as two hundred years ago Canada received thousands of refugees during the American War of Independence – loyalists who wished to retain their links with Britain. In more recent times over 140,000 refugees have found asylum in Canada, as the diagram shows. Because of this record of humane generosity the people of Canada were awarded the Nansen Medal for help to refugees in 1986. As one leading Canadian has said, 'Canada doesn't send people back'.

idea of returning to their homeland and have chosen to settle in their country of asylum. For peasants in a country with plenty of land the arrangements are fairly straightforward. The

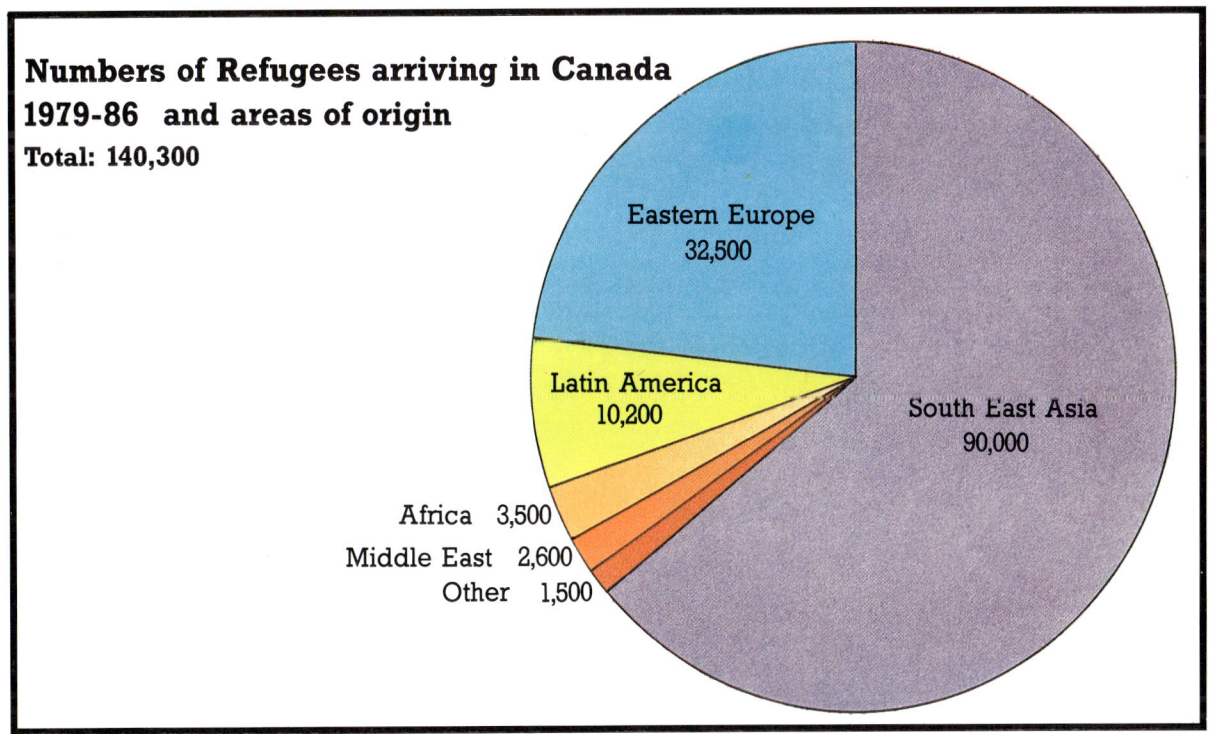

Numbers of Refugees arriving in Canada 1979-86 and areas of origin
Total: 140,300

- Eastern Europe 32,500
- Latin America 10,200
- Africa 3,500
- Middle East 2,600
- Other 1,500
- South East Asia 90,000

5 Help

The need for help

Refugees need a great deal of help. They need legal protection until either they return to their own country or they become citizens of another. They need food, shelter and medicines. They need advice and training for living in a strange land. Individual host countries cannot meet all these needs, especially if they themselves are poor. The plight of refugees would therefore be even more wretched if it were not for the great deal of work undertaken by a number of international and charitable organizations.

We saw in Chapter 2 how UNRRA and the IRO were set up temporarily to deal with the immediate problem of refugees and displaced persons caused by the Second World War. Sadly it soon became evident that the United Nations had to make more detailed arrangements to cope with the problem and so on 1 January 1951 the Office of the United Nations High Commissioner for Refugees (UNHCR) came into existence. The High Commissioner has the following responsibilities:

– to provide legal protection and status for refugees and asylum-seekers as laid down in international conventions;
– to provide material assistance to refugees in need in co-operation with voluntary agencies and governments.

It is important that refugee children, such as these Afghanis in a Pakistani refugee camp, receive an education.

Status and rights

As a citizen a person has certain rights. These vary from country to country, but they generally include protection by the police and the law, and the right to education and health care. When refugees flee they cannot of course claim these rights from their own country. What rights can they expect from their host country? This problem was one of the first to be tackled by UNHCR. In 1951 the Convention on the Status of Refugees was drawn up and by the mid-1980s this had been ratified by 100 countries.

The Convention lists a number of important rights which refugees have in their country of asylum. Most important is what is technically known as 'non-refoulement'. This means that refugees cannot be sent back to their own country against their will. In addition, they must not be discriminated against in their country of asylum: they must be allowed to practise their religion, to educate their children and to seek work as far as possible. They also have the right to a temporary travel permit to visit other countries. One of the most important tasks of

If the refugees are to have any hope of standing on their own feet, they must be allowed to continue working in the trade in which they have been trained.

the UN High Commissioner has been to persuade various governments to make arrangements for putting the terms of the Convention into practice. The United Nations Convention defines a refugee as someone who has 'a well-founded fear of persecution'. However, deciding who is or who is not a genuine refugee is not quite so simple in practice. What of the people who flee because of a well-founded fear, not of persecution but of death by starvation? In practice, since the early 1970s UNHCR has counted such people as refugees. In any case, when thousands of people pour across a frontier it is quite impossible for officials to interview every individual to discover if they all have 'well-founded fears'.

The problem of deciding who is or is not a genuine refugee was dramatically illustrated by an incident in Britain in 1987. At the time there was serious conflict in Sri Lanka between the government and the Tamil minority. In February of that year a group of sixty-four Tamils arrived in Britain seeking asylum on the grounds that their lives would be in danger if they returned home. The British Home Office claimed that fifty-eight of them were 'bogus', that their lives were not in danger and that they had travelled to Britain as illegal immigrants. The Home Secretary said:

> The right of asylum is not given to people who would rather live here because life is more comfortable or more secure than the country to which they belong.

The fifty-eight were taken to Heathrow Airport to be flown back to Sri Lanka. In front of television and newspaper cameras the Tamil men stripped off most of their clothes and refused to board the aeroplane.

The incident provoked much support for the Tamils. It seemed that the British government had less sympathy than many others for the needs of refugees. The incident also showed that British guidelines for dealing with such people were either not being observed properly or were insufficient in scope. In comparison, West Germany, for instance, has a Federal Agency for the Recognition of Foreign Refugees which has dealt with nearly half a million requests for asylum since 1979. The USA has had a Refugee Act since 1980 which, together with a Supreme Court ruling in 1987, makes the rights of refugees seeking asylum in the USA quite clear. Even so, many North American and West European governments have recently become very concerned that people, especially from Asian countries, are seeking asylum when they are not genuine refugees. The danger is that people in the host countries will become very unsympathetic to genuine refugees if people arrive who have no proper claim to that status. On the other hand, it is very hard for a person seeking refuge to prove that he or she had fled in genuine fear.

Tamil refugees at Heathrow Airport, London protesting at being deported to Sri Lanka.

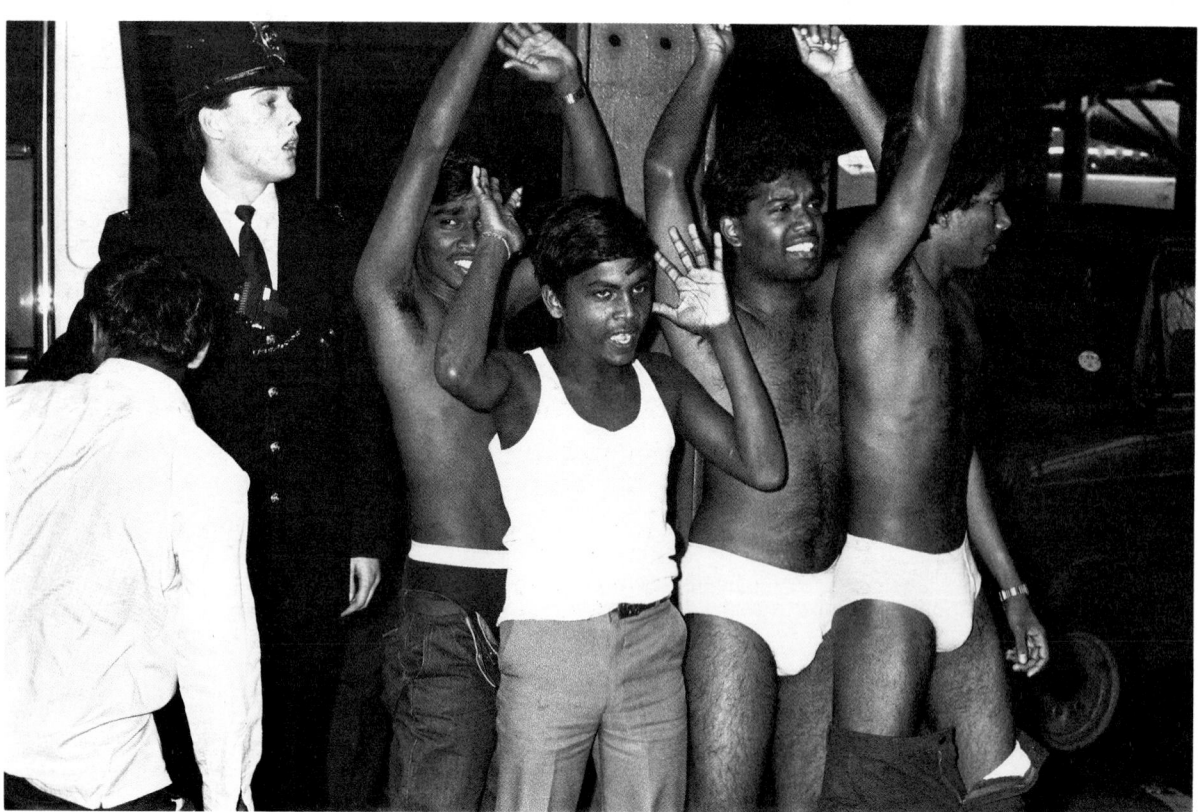

Work of UNHCR

When UNHCR was created it was hoped that it would, one day, not be needed. It was therefore not made a permanent body. But every five years its life has to be renewed as the refugee problem becomes worse rather than better. For example, in 1980 the High Commission spent nearly one hundred times more money than in 1965: $497 million compared with $5 million. Yet UNHCR has no money of its own for supplying refugees with their needs. The High Commissioner must meet his budget each year by appeals for voluntary contributions. Some of these come from governments, some from private organizations and some come from

UNHCR workers vaccinating children at a camp in Sudan. This preventive treatment is part of the overall programme to help refugees.

individuals. This extract from a letter to the Chairman of the British United Nations Association shows how difficult fund-raising is:

UNHCR's budgeted needs in 1986 for its worldwide programmes amount to some $400 million. Less than a third of this amount has so far been raised. Over and above this, I have had to launch on 24 February 1986 a new emergency appeal of $80.6 million for emergency needs in Africa.

Nevertheless, since its creation UNHCR has helped over 25 million people to start a new life. Without the dedicated work of its thousand staff operating from over eight offices throughout the world the plight of refugees would be even grimmer. These officials provide vital help for all the needs of refugees we have already considered: providing shelter and food, making arrangements for refugees to return voluntarily to their own countries and planning settlement in the countries of asylum or immigration to other countries.

Other UN agencies

Although UNHCR is the main United Nations body responsible for refugees, several other UN bodies also undertake important work. We shall look briefly at the work of three of these: UNRWA, UNBRO and UNICEF. In fact they often collaborate in their work. At the New York headquarters of the UN the Secretary-General holds regular meetings with the heads of the various agencies; and in the affected countries a local UN official co-ordinates relief work in the event of a crisis.

The United Nations Relief and Works Agency (UNRWA) was set up in 1949 to help the Palestinian people who became refugees because of the war between Israel and her Arab neighbours. Even when UNHCR was created two years later UNRWA remained a separate body to continue its work. The Agency works under extreme difficulties. In the first place, like UNHCR, it depends on voluntary contributions. Since the early 1970s these have been so insufficient that it has had to reduce its work, sometimes quite drastically. Secondly, the suffering of some of the refugees is made even worse when fighting flares up, as it does every so often. For example, refugees in camps in Beirut, the capital of Lebanon, have been caught in the fighting of the 1980s. The third problem is that the birth-rate is very high so that the number of children to be cared for has been steadily increasing. Families of ten children are quite common. Even so, UNRWA has achieved a great deal over the years. It still manages to supply basic food and, in co-operation with UNESCO (the United Nations Educational, Scientific and Cultural Organization), to provide schooling for the children.

A medical centre in Gaza, run by UNRWA for the Palestinians in the camps.

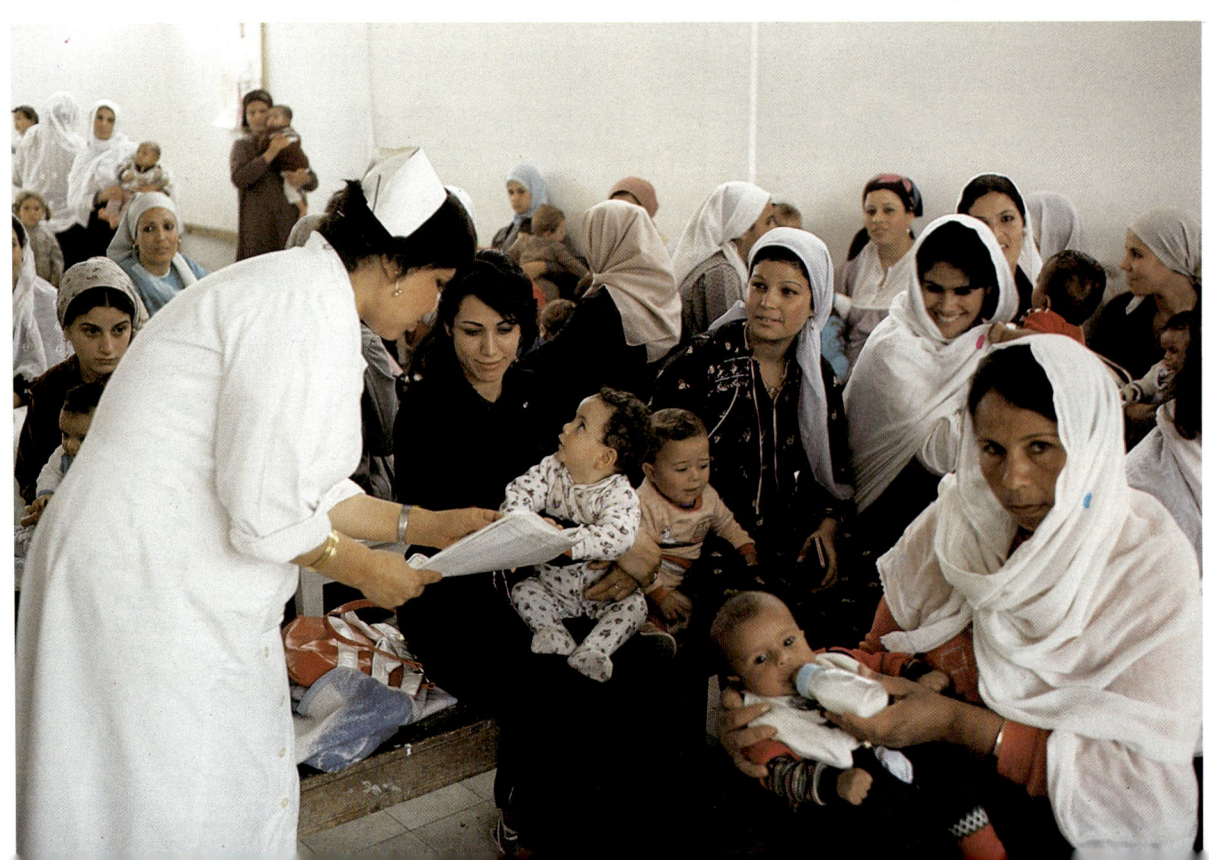

More recently, in 1982, another separate UN refugee organization was created. This is UNBRO – the United Nations Border Relief Organization. Since 1975 the people of Kampuchea have endured the most grievous suffering: a government which slaughtered a large proportion of the population, invasion by Vietnam and civil war. Kampuchean refugees fled from these dangers and are living in the sanctuary of camps just across the border in Thailand. UNBRO was set up to help them.

Another important UN agency helping refugees is UNICEF (United Nations Children's Fund). UNICEF's aim is to try to ensure that children the world over are properly fed, are protected from disease and have at least an elementary education. So many millions lack this basic start in life that UNICEF's programme must be long-term. It is not therefore specifically organized to deal with refugees. On the other hand, it has undertaken very important work for children in refugee camps.

An example of UNICEF's work is the way it

At the Ramallah Training Centre for Women on the West Bank, run by UNRWA, Palestinian women train as teachers.

has helped children during the drought and civil war in Mozambique in southern Africa in the mid-1980s. The following is an extract from a telex sent on 17 March 1987 by the Senior Emergency Officer to the United Kingdom Committee for UNICEF in London:

Just over one million people have lost their homes. People arrive at the displacement camps with virtually no clothes.... In Tete Province it is believed that some of the estimated 70,000 who fled into Malawi are beginning to come back. We will be working with the High Commission for Refugees to welcome people when they return from Malawi. A priority is rehabilitative [reviving] feeding for children because they are generally malnourished.

The work of voluntary bodies

Like UNICEF, there are a number of voluntary organizations which help people suffering from poverty, malnutrition and disease and therefore care for refugees. These include the International Red Cross, the American USA for Africa, the French Médecins sans Frontières (doctors who ignore frontiers), the British Oxfam. Some of these organizations, like the Red Cross, work in many countries. Others concentrate on specific countries: for example, MSF work mainly, but not exclusively, in French-speaking countries in north and west Africa and South East Asia.

In times of crisis several such organizations send help and their work is co-ordinated by the United Nations. For example, the following British agencies are all helping to relieve the suffering caused by the Ethiopian famine: the Red Cross, Save the Children, Christian Aid, CAFOD (Catholic Fund for Overseas Development), War on Want and Oxfam.

A worker for Save the Children Fund weighs a child in the Ban Napho camp in Thailand.

> As well as improving health care, the programme is harnessing the knowledge, resources and initiative of the refugees themselves, giving them back some self-respect and a more meaningful existence.
> *Felicity Cutts, describing a Save the Children fund project in Pakistan*

The practical help these bodies give may be illustrated by the following description from Oxfam. This is the biggest of such organizations working from Britain, with about 700 full-time staff and 20,000 volunteers. The report outlines some work in refugee camps for Ethiopians in Somalia in the early 1980s:

> Initially Oxfam sent a team of doctors and nurses in response to a request from UNICEF to undertake a survey, and advise on and establish nutritional programmes. ... The camp health services are now run by the government's Refugee Health Unit assisted financially by UNHCR and several voluntary agencies. Oxfam has provided feeding kits (mugs, bowls, ladles, etc) for the supplementary feeding organized for malnourished children, pregnant and nursing mothers, and supports the Somali health team working in Saba'ad camp with costs of transport, supplies etc. Salaries are provided for two staff – the Somali training adviser, and the British MCH [maternal and child health] co-ordinator who covers nine camps in the north. Oxfam has also paid for some of the original CHWs [community health workers] to undertake two-year nurses' training. And they are now back working in the camps.

These voluntary organizations exist to help people in dire need. They are charitable and humanitarian, not political, organizations. When they help refugees, should they therefore criticize the government of the country if they believe it to be responsible for these conditions?

Oxfam provides equipment and support for the vast supplementary feeding programme being carried out for the Ethiopians in Somalia. They rely on money from you.

Bob Geldof's forthright and persuasive manner has helped to bring the plight of the starving of Africa to the attention of the world. Here he is performing at Wembley in the Live Aid concert held in July 1985.

If the relief agencies become involved in political controversy, they might be distracted from their task or even be prevented from doing their work by angry governments they have blamed. On the other hand, several leading members of these organizations believe that they must speak out. For example, the Director of Oxfam has declared:

> It would be immoral to ask the public for money without actually telling them about what causes poverty and deprivation. . . . We have to speak about the experiences we have in our work and make those responsible face up to the problems. Asking us to keep quiet is asking us to reverse the whole trend and consistency of our work.

There is one successful organization, however, whose whole work involves it in making political criticisms. This is Amnesty International. Amnesty was set up originally to help 'prisoners of conscience', that is, people who are imprisoned, tortured and threatened with death because of their religious or political beliefs. In recent years Amnesty has extended its work to refugees. It helps individuals to secure asylum, for example, by collecting evidence that they are genuine refugees, whose safety would be in danger if they were forced to return to their own countries.

There has also been one particularly famous individual in the 1980s who was not at all bothered if he offended anyone with his outspoken criticisms. This was the pop musician Bob Geldof. He became very angry about the failure of the governments of the rich countries to give enough help to the starving of Africa. He therefore organized spectacular fund-raising events. Three ventures, called Band Aid, Live Aid and Sport Aid, raised an incredible $200 million.

Again, as with the permanent charities, the money was not specifically for refugees. Nevertheless, it was the films of starving Ethiopian refugees shown on television at the time that made so many millions of people round the world aware of the problem and ready to respond so enthusiastically to Geldof's pleas. Much of the money he raised has in fact been used to help refugees and displaced persons in many parts of Africa.

6 Solutions?

What can you do to help?

> World opinion is a powerful force that greatly assists refugees in their struggle to find a better life.
>
> *UNHCR*

The story of refugees is one of misery and injustice. It is the story of people losing their country, their home and their possessions through no fault of their own. Anyone who is capable of pity, compassion and charity must feel sympathy for these people and this sympathy can be expressed in many positive ways.

At the simplest level we can take the trouble to learn about refugees. This is very easy when a crisis breaks and becomes a news story, but in any case UNHCR offices are always pleased to supply information. So also are many of the voluntary organizations. It is important to learn about refugees and to make your friends aware of the problem. Refugees do not suddenly disappear when there are no dramatic stories on television, yet people can so easily forget. The needs of refugees must be kept alive in our minds and consciences. There is a danger that we will become bored or numbed by constant reminders of human suffering – a modern phrase is 'compassion fatigue' – but true understanding of the subject can help to sustain compassionate sentiments.

We can, of course, show our concern by giving money. As we have seen in Chapter 5 there are plenty of voluntary organizations which can make very good use of it. A little more effort is needed if one is to organize fund-raising activities such as jumble-sales, but they can bring in very useful sums.

Politicians need to be reminded that caring about refugees is important. It is often said that there are no votes in foreign affairs, that citizens are only interested in what politicians say they will do for them. Politicians must be reminded, therefore, that we are not all selfish and that governments of the more fortunate countries are expected to show compassion for the less fortunate. Writing letters and asking questions at meetings can help with this.

Vietnamese refugees who have found asylum in the West. It is up to governments of the rich countries to extend hospitality to refugees.

> The doors to safety are closing against refugees across Europe: in recent years many West European governments have introduced increasingly restrictive measures aimed at preventing or deterring refugees from seeking asylum.
> *Richard Dunstan, Amnesty International*

Nor must we forget that there are refugees in our own country. If we know of refugees in our school, at work or living nearby, small acts of kindness can help to make settling down in a new, strange land a little easier. An interesting American organization Intercultural Mutual Assistance Association, involves refugees in its work to help other refugees.

Working for the cause of refugees can take many forms. Voluntary organizations can always use extra help – serving in an Oxfam shop for example. In recent years an increasing number of people have been offering to work with refugees in the stricken areas of the world. Naturally, people with useful qualifications such as doctors, nurses and teachers are in particular demand. Many of these work heroically in difficult and sometimes dangerous conditions. For example, a British doctor, Pauline Cutting, and nurse, Susan Wighton, tended thousands of refugees under siege in Beirut in 1987, in constant danger from the shooting and the threat of starvation.

There are more than 800 Oxfam shops in Britain. They rely on voluntary help to run them and together they bring in a profit of around £15 million.

Plastic mugs provided by Save the Children Fund being handed out at the Kombolcha Transit Camp in Ethiopia. Organizations like SCF and Oxfam rely on your donations to fund the work they do all over the world.

Reducing suffering

It is easy to dismiss our own responsibility to help with the problem. The huge size of it can readily bring on an overwhelmingly defeatist attitude. We can so readily assume that no individual's efforts can really reduce this mountain of human misery by any measurable amount. But if human beings took this view of all major problems that confront them, very little would be achieved.

Individual help does count, and for two reasons. In the first place even a small contribution can help another human being: a few pence will provide a plastic mug or a dose of vaccine. An individual's help multiplied hundreds of thousands of times has considerable effect. Secondly, the more that feelings of compassion, tolerance and humanity can be spread throughout the world, the more unthinkable it will become for human beings to be allowed to suffer as refugees do. In the words of the eighteenth-century Irish writer and politician, Edmund Burke, 'The only thing necessary for the triumph of evil is for good men to do nothing.'

Much more could be achieved in alleviating the wretchedness of refugees: more money and more volunteers could improve conditions in the camps, more refugees could be allowed to settle in the wealthier countries. One improvement would be a revision of the system of detention. Some refugees are kept in prison conditions for months in countries where they are seeking asylum while the authorities decide whether they will allow them to settle. This unnecessary misery could be considerably relieved.

Tackling the roots of the problem

How much better it would be if there were no refugees at all. To achieve this the world must eliminate the fear which prompts people to flee from their homes. There are three basic causes: famine, war and oppression.

The elimination of fear of famine is the easiest to tackle. Experts working for the various international and voluntary organizations can predict when a famine is likely to strike. North America and western Europe produce much more food than they can eat. Famine can therefore theoretically be prevented. It needs the following: information about the climatic and rainfall patterns, generosity on the part of the countries with food surpluses, improved transport to convey food to endangered areas, and the agreement of the governments of the threatened people to accept this charity.

The threat of famine is often the result of natural disasters such as flood, drought or pests like locusts. The problem is complicated if food production is affected by war. It would be quite unrealistic to expect the world to be rid of war in the forseeable future but what we might hope for is a greater readiness on the part of armies to keep the suffering of the civilian population to a minimum. Armies which deliberately maltreat civilians should be clearly condemned, and where wars are affecting civilians, the armies involved should give assistance to relief agencies to help protect them. If people can be given a certain sense of security even in war conditions, the risks of staying may be less than the risks of becoming refugees.

Just as governments and armies may be shamed by critical publicity into more humane behaviour in times of war, so in times of peace oppressive governments may be persuaded to mend their ways and respect human rights. Perhaps through persistent and accurate complaints to the right quarters, the number of victims of torture and wrongful imprisonment will decline. Fewer people will therefore feel the necessity to flee for fear of becoming just such a victim. For example, since the end of the military dictatorship in Argentina in 1984, thousands of refugees have returned to their homeland.

That there are perhaps as many as 15 million refugees in the world is a disgrace to humankind, and humankind must be shamed into curing this political and moral epidemic.

Long-term assistance is as important as short-term aid. This health supervisor, funded by Save the Children Fund, is training Afghani refugee women to be midwives.

A camp being established by UNHCR in the Red Sea Province of Sudan.

Glossary

Asylum Place of safety.
Convention In international law, an agreement signed by a number of states.
Displaced person Similar to a refugee but less precise in meaning. Often used today to describe a person who has fled from his or her home but not to another country.
Host country Country receiving a refugee.
IRO International Relief Organization, set up in 1947.
Non-refoulement Technical term in international law referring to the right of refugees not to be forced against their will to return to the country from which they have fled.
Persecute To oppress, especially because of race or religion.
Repatriation Return of refugees to their own country on a voluntary basis.

Sanctuary Place of safety.
United Nations International organization consisting of a 'family' of agencies. It was established in 1945 to try to reduce conflict and war.
UNBRO United Nations Border Relief Organization set up to assist Kampuchean refugees in Thailand.
UNHCR United Nations High Commission for Refugees set up in 1951 to provide legal protection and material assistance for refugees.
UNICEF United Nations Children's Fund which aids education and child and maternal health in developing countries.
UNRWA United Nations Relief and Works Agency set up in 1949 to help Palestinian refugees.

Picture Acknowledgements

The publishers would like to thank the following for the illustrations used in this book: BBC Hulton Picture Library 10; Bridgeman Art Library 8; Jill Brown (Save the Children Fund) 19; N. Cooper and J. Hammond (Save the Children Fund) 42; Billie Love 9; Oxfam 37, 40; Rex Features 32; Save the Children Fund 29, 37; Topham 14, 38; Penny Tweedie, cover, frontispiece, 21 (top); United Nations High Commission for Refugees 7, 17, 21 (bottom), 22, 23, 26, 27, 30, 31, 33, 39, 43, 47; United Nations Relief and Works Agency 16, 28, 34, 35; Mike Wells (Save the Children Fund) 24, 25, 41.

Further information

These organizations will help you learn more about refugees and what can be done to help them. They will provide newsletters, worksheets and information packs.

British Refugee Council,
Bondway House,
3/9 Bondway,
London SW8 1SJ

Christian Aid,
P.O. Box No.1,
London SW9 8BH

Christian Aid,
201 Stanton Street,
Fort Erie,
Ontario L2A 3N8,
CANADA

Community Aid Abroad,
541 George Street,
Sydney,
NSW 2000,
AUSTRALIA

Oxfam,
242 Banbury Road,
OX2 7DZ

Save the Children Fund,
Mary Datchelor House,
17 Grove Lane,
London SE5 8RD

UNHCR Branch Office,
36 Westminster Palace Gardens,
Artillery Row,
London SW1P 1RR

UNHCR,
280 Albert Street, Suite 401,
Ottawa,
Ontario K1P 5G8,
CANADA

UNHCR,
10 Moore Street,
Canberra
A.C.T. 2600
AUSTRALIA

UNRWA Headquarters (Vienna),
Vienna International Centre,
P.O. Box 700,
1400 Vienna
AUSTRIA

Books to read

Ashworth, Georgina *The Boat People and the Road People: Refugees in Vietnam, Laos and Cambodia* (Quartermaine House, Windmill Road, Sunbury, Middlesex, 1979)

Shaming the World: *The Needs of Women Refugees* (Change/World University Service, 20 Compton Terrace, London N1 2UN, 1984)

Wilson, Francesca *Aftermath* (Penguin, 1947)

Gibb, Christopher *Food or Famine?* (Wayland (Publishers) Ltd, 1987)

Magazines and pamphlets

Amnesty 'No Entry' (June/July issue, 1987, Amnesty International)

Exile (newsletter, British Refugee Council)

Palestine Refugees Today (quarterly journal, UNRWA)

Refugee Children Around the World (work booklet, UNHCR)

Refugees (illustrated monthly magazine, UNHCR)

Settling for a Future: Proposals for a British policy on refugees (British Refugee Council, 1987)

Information packs

Africa's Refugees (British Refugee Council)
Refugees in Need (UNHCR)

Index

The numbers in **bold** refer to the pictures.

Afghanis **19, 30, 42**
Afghanistan 6, 18–20
Africa 6, 20–21
Allies 12
Amnesty International 38
Angola 29
Arabs 15–17
Armenians **9**

Bartók, Béla 9
Beirut 34
Berlin Wall 23
Britain 10, 11, 31–2

CAFOD 36
Canada 29
China 13, 17
Central America 6, 18
Christian Aid 36
Convention on the Status of Refugees 31
Cutting, Pauline 40

displaced persons 12
Djibouti 20, 28

education 26
Einstein, Albert 9
El Salvador 18, **47**
Ethiopia 20–21, 25, 36, 38, **41**
  Eritrea 20
  Tigre 20
  Wollo 20
Ethiopians **7, 21, 22,** 23, 24, 28, **37**

famine 6, 15, 20, 31
First World War 9
food 7, 25, 26, 30, 42
France 12, 17

Gandhi, Mahatma 13
Geldof, Bob 38, **38**
Germans 12
Germany 10, 11–12
Guatemala 18
Guatemalans **23,** 26–7, **26**

Hindus 13, **14**
Honduras 18, **47**

Hong Kong 13, **17,** 18
Huguenots 8

India 13
Intercultural Mutual Assistance Association 40
International Red Cross 36
International Refugee Organization (IRO) 13, 30
Iran 6, **9,** 18–19
Israel 15–17, 28

Japan 13
Jesus Christ **8,** 9
Jews 10, **10,** 15–17
Jordan 17, 28, **28**

Kampuchea 35

League of Nations 9–10
Lebanon 17, 34
Louis XIV 8

Malawi 35
Médecins sans Frontières 36
medicine 25, 30
Mexico 18, **23,** 26–7, **26, 27**
Middle East 6
Mozambicans 23
Mozambique 21, 35
Muhammad 9
Muslims 13, 18

Nansen, Fridtjof 9–10
Namibians 29
Nazism 10, 15
Nicaragua 18

Oxfam 36, **36,** 38, **40, 41**

Palestine 10, 15–17
Palestinians 15–17, 28, **28,**
  Gaza 16–17, **16,** 28, **34**
  West Bank 16–17, **35**
Pakistan 6, 13, **14,** 18–20, **19, 30**
Poles 12
prisoners of war 11–12

reception camps 24
refugee camps 25
Russians 12

Save the Children Fund 10, 36, **36, 41,** 42
Second World War 11, 30
self-sufficiency 27
Sikhs **14**
slave labour 11–12
South Africa 21, 23
South East Asia 6, 18
Somalia 20, **21,** 22, 24, 25, 28, 36
Soviet Union 11, 12, 18–20
Sri Lanka 31–2
Sudan **7,** 20, **21,** 22, 29, **33**
Supreme Headquarters Allied Expeditionary Force (SHAEF) 13
Syria 17

Taiwan 13
Tamils 32, **32**
Tanzania 29
Thailand 35, **36**

Ugandans 29
UNBRO 34, 35
UNESCO 34
UNHCR 30, 33–4, 36, 39
UNICEF 34, 35, 36
United Nations 6, 13, 14, 15, 18, 29, 30–31
United Nations Relief and Rehabilitation Administration (UNRRA) 13, 30
United States of America 10, 12, 32
UNRWA 16–17, 34
USA for Africa 36

Vietnam 17–18
Vietnamese 17–18, 23, **23,** 29, **39**

war 6, 12, 15, 19, 20, 21, 42
War on Want 36
water 25, **25**
West Germany 32

A camp in Honduras for refugees from El Salvador.